X3

9/05

AMERICA'S
MOUNTAINS

BY FRANK STAUB

MONDO

For Red, Toni, Joshua, April, and Jonathan . . .
and for Galen Rowell (1940-2002):
Forever an inspiration—F.S.

With special thanks to our consultant Jean S. Cline,
Professor of Geoscience at the University of Nevada
in Las Vegas

Text copyright © 2003 by Frank Staub

Illustrations on pp. 7 and 11 copyright © 2003 by Annette Cyr under
exclusive license to MONDO Publishing

Photographs copyright © 2003 by Frank Staub under exclusive license to
MONDO Publishing, with the exception of the following:
pp. 12-13: © NPS Photo by Kepa Maly Hawaii Volcanoes National Park;
p. 16: © E. Cooper/Robertstock.com; p. 17: © R. Lamb/Robertstock.com;
p. 19: © Scott Lopez/NPS Photo; pp. 30-31: © R. Kord/Robertstock.com

For information contact:
MONDO Publishing
980 Avenue of the Americas
New York, NY 10018

Visit our web site at http://www.mondopub.com

Printed in China

03 04 05 06 07 08 09   9 8 7 6 5 4 3 2 1

ISBN 1-59034-870-2 (HC) ISBN 1-59034-872-9 (PB)

Designed by Annette Cyr

Library of Congress Cataloging-in-Publication Data

Staub, Frank J.
    America's mountains / by Frank Staub.
      p. cm.
    Contents: How high is a mountain? -- Building up -- Tearing down -- Rain, wind, and
snow -- Life zones -- Horns, hooves, fur, and feathers -- Mountains of change.
    Summary: Explores the mountains of America, discussing what a mountain is, the
different types of mountains and how they are formed, mountain climates, and plant and
animal life of the mountains.
    ISBN 1-59034-870-2 (hc) -- ISBN 1-59034-872-9
    1. Mountains--United States--Juvenile literature. [1. Mountains.] I. Title.

QH104.S76 2002
551.43'2'0973--dc21
                                                          2003044934

CONTENTS

INTRODUCTION

Mt. Moran, Grand Teton Range, Wyoming

Few things are more striking than a tall mountain surrounded by clouds and crowned with snow. Painters have long used mountains to show nature's beauty. In the words of the 19th-century art critic John Ruskin, "Mountains are the beginning and the end of all natural scenery."

Mountains also play a role in what people believe. The ancient Greeks believed their gods lived on Mt. Olympus. Mt. Fuji, the tallest peak in Japan, is the most sacred place to the Buddhist and Shinto religions. Jews and Christians believe that god appeared to the prophet Moses on a mountain. According to John Muir, father of the American conservation movement, climbing a mountain is a way to "wash your spirit clean."

People also look to the mountains to help their civilizations grow. Necessary minerals are mined from mountains. Most of the lumber and paper we use comes from trees in mountain forests. Mountain streams are an important source of water. And mountains are great places to have fun. Skiing, hiking, mountain biking, fishing, and sightseeing are a few of the ways people enjoy America's mountains.

However, mountains can also cause problems. They are natural borders that keep people apart. They form barriers to travel. Mountain weather can be dangerous. And America's mountains caused hardships for the early settlers who tried to cross them.

Backpackers make camp before climbing a mountain in the San Juan Range in Colorado.

CHAPTER ONE

How High Is a Mountain?

Which one is the mountain and which one is the hill?

What is a mountain? And how high is it compared to a hill? For a piece of land to be called a mountain, its high point or summit must be only a small area and be at least 1,000 feet (304.8 m) above the lowlands, or lower areas surrounding it. However, there are exceptions. Although some summits in South Dakota's Black Hills are over 1,000 feet above the lowlands, they are still called hills. And not one summit in the Boston Mountains of Arkansas stands more than 1,000 feet higher than the lowlands, so they aren't actually mountains. But a true mountain must rise at least 1,000 feet above the surrounding area.

A mountain's official elevation (e-luh-VAY-shun) is the vertical distance from sea level to summit. Mauna Kea (MOW-nuh KEE-uh) in Hawaii has an elevation of 13,796 feet (4,205 m) above sea level. However, it towers roughly 32,000 feet (9,754 m) above its base on the Pacific Ocean floor. If mountains were measured from base to summit, Mauna Kea would be the world's tallest. Instead, that honor goes to Mt. Everest in Nepal at 29,035 feet (8,850 m) above sea level. However, Mauna Kea's neighbor, Mauna Loa (MOW-nuh LOW-uh), is the largest mountain on Earth if you combine both its height and the amount of area it covers.

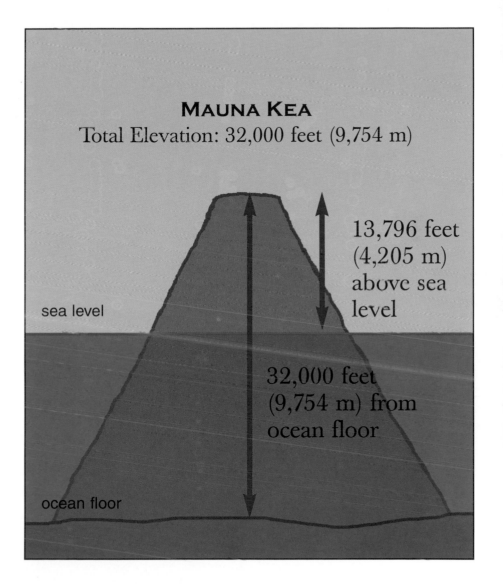

MAUNA KEA
Total Elevation: 32,000 feet (9,754 m)

13,796 feet (4,205 m) above sea level

sea level

32,000 feet (9,754 m) from ocean floor

ocean floor

More than half of Mauna Kea, in Hawaii, is underwater.

7

A mountain range may be one ridge or many closely spaced ridges and peaks.

Mountains often occur close together in what are called mountain ranges. A group of mountain ranges may be part of a mountain system. New Hampshire's White Mountains and the Great Smoky Mountains of Tennessee and North Carolina are two of many ranges in the Appalachian (ap-uh-LAY-shun) Mountain System. Out west, the Rocky Mountain System contains over 100 ranges including Wyoming's Grand Teton Range and Colorado's Sawatch (suh-WACH) Range. Farther west, the Pacific Mountain System consists of California's Sierra Nevada Range; the Cascade Range in Washington, Oregon, and California; the Coast Mountains of British Columbia; the Coast Ranges along much of the Pacific Coast; and the Alaska and Aleutian (uh-LOO-shun) ranges.

Just as a group of mountain ranges together make up a mountain system, a few mountain systems together make up a cordillera (kor-dee-YER-uh). A cordillera is a continent's principal group of mountains. Mexico's Sierra Madre Mountains, together with the Pacific Mountain System, the Rockies, and many small ranges in between, make up the North American Cordillera.

Broad, flat areas called plateaus (plat-OWZ) are often associated with mountains. A plateau has at least one side that is high and steep. Plateaus often occur between the lowlands and the foothills. Foothills are the hills at the base of a mountain range. The Colorado Plateau in northern Arizona and southern Utah stands between the Rocky Mountain foothills and the southwestern desert lowlands.

Some mountains develop as the surface of the Earth is built up. Others appear as the Earth's surface is worn away. The way a mountain forms determines the type of mountain it is. There are five main kinds of mountains: folded mountains, volcanoes, fault-block mountains, dome mountains, and erosion mountains.

CHAPTER TWO

Building Up

The Southern Appalachian Mountains are folded mountains.

Mountains are formed by the changing of the Earth's crust. Geologists (jee-OL-uh-jists), scientists who study the Earth and how it was formed, tell us that the crust is the upper part of the lithosphere (LITH-uh-sfeer), or the Earth's skin. Unlike the skin of an orange, the lithosphere is not one unbroken piece. It is more like the shell of a hard-boiled egg when it's been cracked. The cracks separate the lithosphere into plates. Each plate has a name. The North American continent is part of the North American Plate.

Beneath the lithosphere lies the Earth's asthenosphere (as-THEN-uh-sfeer). Most of the asthenosphere is nearly solid, but some is so hot that it has melted into a liquid called magma. The asthenosphere flows like very thick molasses.

Both the magma and semisolid rock in the asthenosphere move slowly, like currents in a thick, underground sea. The plates of the lithosphere float on these deep currents somewhat like ice floats on water. Each year, the floating plates move an inch or two at most. These slow movements are called plate tectonics (PLAYT tek-TON-iks).

At the places where two lithosphere plates meet, one of three things happens: One plate may slide beneath the other plate, the plates may slide past each other, or the plates may move away from each other. These three events are the main causes of most mountain building.

If one plate slides beneath another, some of the crust covering the top plate may crumple like folds in a loose tablecloth. If the folds are large enough, they form folded mountains. Between 300 and 225 million years ago, the African Plate slid beneath the North American Plate. This caused the North American Plate to crumple. The result was the folded mountains we now call the Southern Appalachian Mountains.

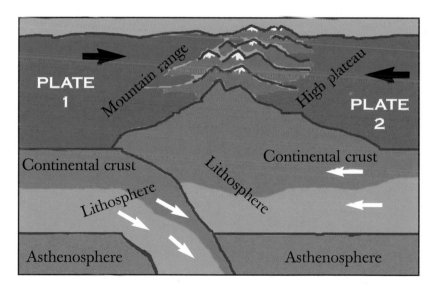

When two plates come together, the force can cause the top plate to crumple and form folded mountains.

Lava erupts from a hole, called a crater, in a Hawaiian volcano...

Then, about 200 million years ago, the African and North American plates reversed directions. To this day, they are moving away from each other. The area between the two plates is on the floor of the Atlantic Ocean. As the plates continue to move apart, magma oozes up from inside the Earth to fill the space between them.

Magma that has reached the Earth's surface is called lava (LA-vuh). Sometimes lava spreads out flat on the surface to form plains. Thicker lava piles up into cone-shaped mountains called volcanoes (vol CAY-nowz). For millions of years, lava has flowed out from between the African and North American plates. This lava then hardened into new crust, forming a 10,000-mile-long (16,093-km-long) chain of underwater volcanoes called the Mid-Atlantic Ridge. This string of volcanoes is the world's longest mountain range.

Along America's West Coast, from San Francisco southward into Mexico, the North American Plate is sliding to the southeast. Right beside it, the Pacific Plate is sliding to the northwest. But the sliding isn't smooth. The two plates' ragged edges snag against each other and then move again suddenly. These movements cause the Earth's crust to crack.

The view from Mt. Whitney looks over the Sierra Nevada
Range, which is a series of fault-block mountains.

A crack in the Earth's crust is called a fault if the ground on either side of the crack moves. When the area around the crack moves suddenly, the crust vibrates, causing an earthquake. Movement of the North American Plate has caused hundreds of faults throughout western North America. Pieces of crust along many of the faults have been pushed up to form fault-block mountains, such as the Sierra Nevada Range in central California. One of these fault-block mountains is Mt. Whitney. Standing 14,495 feet (4,418 m) above sea level, Mt. Whitney is the tallest peak in the United States outside of Alaska. Alaska, however, has 16 mountains that rise higher than Mt. Whitney, including North America's tallest peak, Mt. McKinley (20,320 feet [6,194 m]), which also occurs along a fault.

One hundred sixty smaller fault-block mountain ranges are scattered throughout most of Nevada and parts of Oregon, California, and Utah. In between these ranges lie low areas called basins. The resulting landscape is called basin and range.

Plate movements along North America's West Coast have also produced a series of small, folded, faulted, and volcanic mountains called the Coast Ranges, which run from southern Canada to southern California.

Basin and range landscapes can also be found in New Mexico and in Arizona, pictured here.

Mt. Rainier, part of the Cascade Range, is a big, active volcano in Washington.

Along America's Pacific Northwest Coast, the small Juan de Fuca Plate (WAN day FYOO-ka PLAYT) dips beneath the North American Plate. As the Juan de Fuca Plate gets squeezed beneath the North American Plate, heat and pressure melt the upper part of the plate into magma. As the magma builds it rises up through the lithosphere and flows out as lava onto the surface in Washington, Oregon, and northern California. The result is a chain of volcanoes called the Cascade Range. California's Mt. Shasta, Oregon's Mt. Hood, and Washington's Mt. Rainier are all in the Cascades.

Most of the Cascade Range volcanoes show little activity. However, in 1980, Washington's Mt. St. Helens erupted. Hot gases, rocks, and volcanic ash spewed from the crater. Volcanic ash is lava that has been blown apart by exploding gas, turning it into a fine, gray powder. The ash cloud from Mt. St. Helens was so large it was visible from space!

Over the centuries, many Cascade Range volcanoes have erupted explosively like Mt. St. Helens. But eruptions aren't always so dramatic. Some are more gentle and quiet, with lava flowing down the volcanoes' sides in streams.

The eruption of Mt. St. Helens killed 59 people and knocked down enough trees to build 300,000 homes.

Where do you think the steam is coming from in this picture of Yellowstone National Park?

All of the volcanoes in Hawaii, including Mauna Kea, were formed by non-explosive eruptions. Unlike most mountain ranges, Hawaii's volcanoes are far away from the unstable boundaries between plates. They were formed at a hot spot, which is the area above a mass of magma that moves up from inside the Earth and breaks through weak spots in the Earth's crust. As the Pacific Plate passed over this hot spot, magma broke through the plate at different places. At each new place, lava poured from the crust to create a volcano. Volcanoes grew and eventually rose above the ocean's surface to make islands.

This process continued for thousands of years, creating the Hawaiian chain of volcanic islands. It continues today. Kilauea, a crater on the side of Mauna Loa, still sends out lava flows. And just east, a new volcano is building on the ocean floor. Some day it, too, will likely become an island.

Yellowstone National Park sits over another hot spot. Here, volcanoes from the past are no longer active. But the pool of magma they grew from is just two miles below the surface. As water from rain and melting snow seeps into Yellowstone's soil, it flows into cracks in hot rocks that heat it to the boiling point. Hot water and steam then rise back to the surface and emerge as bubbling, steaming hot springs.

Yellowstone's mountains are part of the Rocky Mountain System. However, most Rocky Mountain ranges weren't formed by hot spots. Rather, they developed from plate movements, which caused folding and faulting at weak points in the crust. Still, like many mountain systems, the Rockies are made up of more than one kind of mountain. As the Rockies rose up, magma crept into some of the folds and faults. Then, in a few places, the magma flowed onto the surface to form plateaus and mountains such as Colorado's San Juan Range (SAN WAN RAYNJ), which is part of the Rocky Mountain System.

After a dual eruption of Mauna Loa and Kilauea, a lava river flows down the volcanoes' sides.

Sometimes magma pushes the rock layers that are above it up into a dome shape. The magma then hardens to form a hard core deep within a dome mountain. New York's Adirondack (ad-uh-RON-dak) Mountains are the solid cores of a great range of dome mountains that existed over 600 million years ago. But what happened to these mountains? Why do only the cores remain? How did the rock layers that once covered the mountain cores disappear? We'll find out in the next chapter.

When basalt lava cools and hardens, it may form straight columns with flat sides, as it does here at Devil's Postpile National Monument in the Sierra Nevada Range, California.

Rocks
of Heat and
Change

The Earth's crust is made of rock, and a common rock found on land is granite (GRAN-it). Granite is a kind of rock known as igneous (IG-nee-us) rock. Igneous rocks come from either lava or magma that cools and becomes solid.

Rocks are made of minerals. Quartz (KWORTZ) and feldspar (FELD-spar) are the two most abundant minerals that come from the magma that forms granite. Granitic magma cools and turns into rock very slowly, deep in the Earth.

Sometimes the same kind of magma that forms granite flows up onto the Earth's surface as lava. The lava cools quickly to form other kinds of igneous rocks. Although these lava rocks contain the same minerals as granite, they look different. The quick cooling gives them a smoother texture than the rough-looking, slow-cooled granite.

Basalt (BA-zult), another igneous rock, forms from lava that contains a large amount of iron. Iron, along with other elements, gives basalt a much darker color than granite. Basalt is the most common lava rock in Hawaii, the Pacific Northwest, and the Earth's crust beneath the ocean basins.

Heat from lava and magma can change the appearance of nearby rock, and so can pressure. This pressure can come from tons of overlying rock pressing down on it, or from movements of the Earth's crust against it. Rock that changes due to heat or pressure is called metamorphic (met-uh-MOR-fik) rock.

CHAPTER THREE

Tearing Down

A swift mountain stream in the Great Smoky Mountains picks up sediment as it flows over the land, gradually causing erosion.

Mountains seem to last forever. American author Nathaniel Hawthorne called them the "earth's undecaying monuments." But mountains do decay . . . and in time they disappear. Consider the Rocky Mountains of Colorado. They formed about 65 million years ago. But more than 200 million years before that, other big mountain chains stood near where the Colorado Rockies are today. Geologists call them the Ancestral (an-SES-trul) Rockies. Very slowly, erosion (i-ROW-zhun) broke down those ancient ranges into sand, gravel, and sediments (SED-i-ments). Erosion is the wearing away of rock and soil by water, wind, ice, and other forces.

Water is the great shaper of most landforms. The water in streams picks up sediments and forces them to act like sandpaper, scraping and moving the rocks and soil on the stream bottom. In this way, a stream will slowly erode a landscape until a valley forms.

Ice is another important cause of mountain erosion. In places with long, cold winters, all the snow may not melt during the summer. These mountain areas become what is referred to as snowfields. As each winter passes, another layer of snow falls on top of the snowfield's layers from previous winters. In time, the snow turns to

Rocks

Formed from Sediments

As granite and other rocks erode, they turn into sediments such as sand and fine, mud-forming particles called silt. Streams wash the sand and silt into lakes and oceans where, together with sediments made up of the shells of tiny animal organisms, they form thick layers. Centuries pass, and the lower sediments become cemented together to form solid rock. Layers of sand turn to sandstone, silt becomes shale, and the shell sediments form limestone. Types of rocks such as these, which are formed from sediments, are called sedimentary (sed-i-MENT-ery) rocks. Sedimentary rocks may also form from the sediments dropped by streams, melting ice, or wind.

Like most of the glaciers in Montana's Glacier National Park, this one is almost gone.

ice. As the ice thickens, it may move downhill in the form of a glacier (GLAY-shur), or large mass of flowing ice. Mountain glaciers usually follow valleys already cut by streams.

A glacier advances down a mountain as snow and ice build up during the winter. But in the summer, the glacier melts. When there are many warm years in a row, a glacier isn't able to build up enough mass during the winter to make up for what melted in the summer. If the warm weather continues, the glacier disappears.

At different times in Earth's history, the climate has been both hotter and colder than it is now. The time periods when the climate was much colder are called ice ages. The Earth has experienced several different ice ages throughout its history. Some scientists say the last ice age ended 10,000 years ago. Others say we are going through its final stages now. In either case, when the most recent ice age was at its height, huge glaciers filled mountain valleys throughout North America.

You can still find glaciers in the mountains of Alaska and in the Cascades, Olympics, and northern Rockies. But the glaciers are getting smaller. In fact, all over the world, glaciers are shrinking as the Earth warms up.

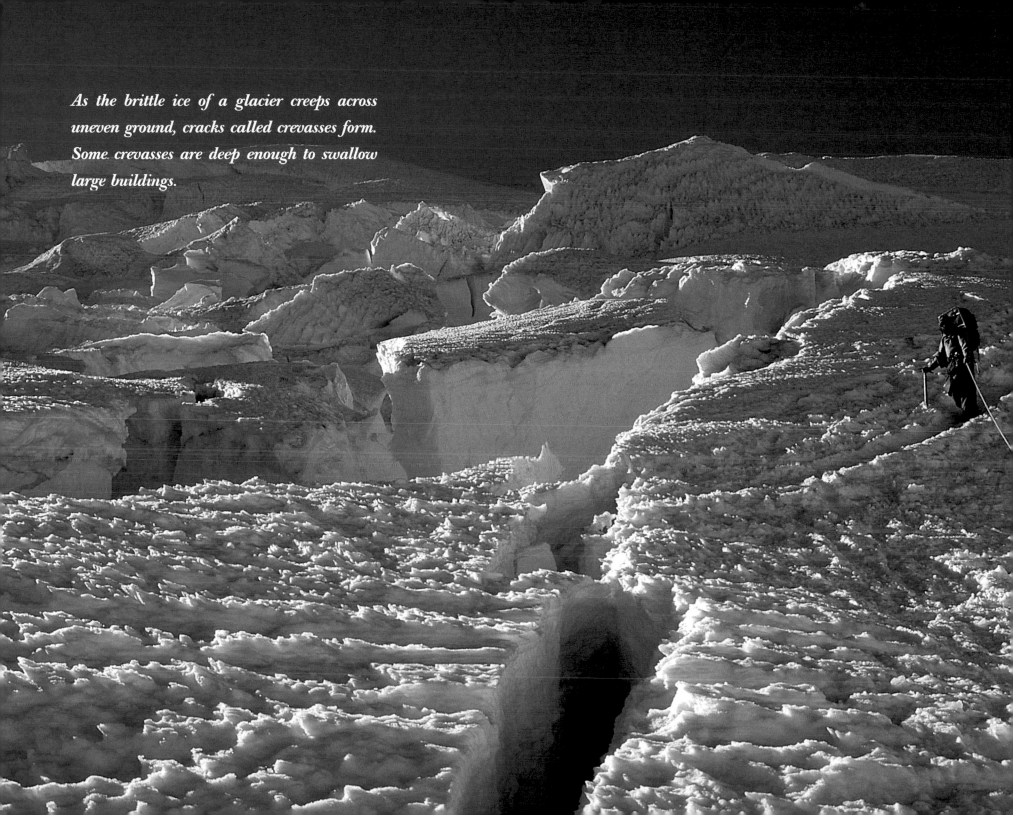

As the brittle ice of a glacier creeps across uneven ground, cracks called crevasses form. Some crevasses are deep enough to swallow large buildings.

A glacier carved out this U-shaped valley in Colorado. The rock piles below the lake are moraines.

Most of the glaciers from America's past are gone. But the evidence that they existed covers America's mountains. As a glacier creeps down a mountain, rocks and other sediments from the sides of the valley it moves through fall onto the ice. Sediments also become frozen into the glacier's bottom and sides. As the glacier melts, it drops its load of sediment in piles called moraines (moor-AYNZ).

Sediments embedded in the sides and bottom of a moving glacier grind away at the land, smoothing the rough surfaces. Eventually, the glacier changes the valley's shape from that of a stream-carved "V," to a gentle "U." U-shaped glacial valleys occur throughout the Sierra Nevadas, Rockies, Cascades, Northern Appalachians, and Olympics. Moraines left by the retreating ice often dot these valleys.

You can tell a mountain range's age from the way it looks. For example, ranges in the Rocky Mountain System are more jagged than those in the Appalachians because the Rockies are younger. The 60 million years since the Rockies formed hasn't been enough time for erosion to wear them down as much. But 200 million years of erosion have left the Appalachians smooth and rolling.

Colorado's Elk Range in the Rocky Mountain System (above) is higher and more jagged than North Carolina's Great Smoky Range in the Appalachian Mountain System (below). This is due to erosion.

The Canadian Shield's rock core lies exposed in Algonquin Provincial Park in Canada. Most of the sediments have been removed by ice.

The Appalachians' great age is also why they aren't as high as most western ranges. At 6,684 feet (2,037 m) above sea level, North Carolina's Mt. Mitchell is the highest peak in the Appalachian Range. Yet in Colorado alone there are 54 summits over 14,000 feet (4,267 m).

When a mountain range has been completely eroded away, it may leave behind a shield. A shield is the hard rock core left after water and ice break down a mountain range or other landform and carry the sediments away. A shield lasts a long time; it is part of the foundation rock that lies under a continent.

Half of Canada and parts of the northern United States are covered by large areas of igneous and metamorphic rock called the Canadian Shield. The Canadian Shield was once the base of a great mountain range that existed over 600 million years ago. Today, New York's Adirondack Mountains stand as high points at the southeastern end of the Canadian Shield. Water and ice have long since removed the many layers of rock that once covered these dome mountains.

Mountains and structures that are similar to mountains may form when a plateau is eroded. After many thousands of years, some parts of the plateau may remain standing. These areas may be made of rock that is harder and more resistant to erosion than the rock in other parts of the plateau. Or the remains of a plateau may somehow have been protected from the full force of rushing streams and moving glaciers.

If a section of an old plateau has a summit that is small and sides that are sloping rather than straight up and down, then it is called a hill or mountain. The Catskill Mountains in New York are erosion mountains formed from a plateau. However, if an old plateau has a flat top that covers a large area and has at least one very steep side, it is called a mesa (MAY-suh). If the flat summit is small and the sides are very steep, it is called a butte (BYOOT). As mesas erode and get smaller, they may become buttes. The dry regions of southern Utah and northern Arizona are famous for their mesas and buttes, which are cut from the colorful sedimentary rocks of the Colorado Plateau.

Some parts of the Colorado Plateau were eroded away while other parts remained standing as buttes and mesas. Can you find an example of both a butte and a mesa here?

CHAPTER FOUR

Rain, Wind, and Snow

Mountains are said to create their own weather. Here, a storm is building over the Front Range in Colorado's Rocky Mountains.

Mountains are colder and wetter than the lowlands that surround them. To understand why, look to the air. Air contains water in the form of a gas, called water vapor. As warm air rises up a mountainside, it cools off. Cool air can't hold as much water vapor as warm air. So as the air rises and cools, its water vapor turns into tiny liquid water drops. These water drops combine to become clouds, which then drop rain or snow on the mountains. The water from rain and melting snow forms streams. These streams run down the mountains and combine to form rivers that flow through the foothills and on to flat land. A river and the streams that flow into it are called a drainage system.

The high area separating two drainage systems is called a divide. A low point in a divide where people can cross over to the other side of the mountains is called a pass.

Mountains may influence the weather in the lowlands. In North America, most of the wind comes from the west. As winds reach a range of mountains, they drop much of their moisture as rain and snow. Thus, the windward side of a mountain range, or the side facing the wind, is often wet. After these winds cross the mountains, they contain less moisture. So the mountains' leeward side, or the side facing away from the wind, receives much less rain and snow. It lies in what is called the mountains' rain shadow.

Can you find the drainage system, a divide, and a pass in this photograph?

CHAPTER FIVE

Life Zones

Can you tell which of these Colorado Rocky Mountain trees are deciduous and which are coniferous?

Most of America's mountains are covered with forests, and most of America's forests are in the mountains. These forests contain two main kinds of trees: deciduous (dee-SID-yoo-us) and coniferous (kon-IH-fer-us).

Deciduous tree leaves turn color and drop off in the time between growing seasons, which is generally autumn. Deciduous or broad-leaved trees have leaves that are usually wide and flat. Maple, oak, aspen, and birch are common deciduous trees in mountainous areas. Their seeds are in flowers, fruits, or nuts that grow on the trees.

Most coniferous trees are evergreen plants, which means they keep their needles or scales through the winter. Coniferous tree leaves are shaped either like needles or like scales on a fish. Pine, fir, spruce, and juniper are common coniferous trees. Their seeds are in cones that grow on the trees.

Because mountain weather gets colder and wetter at higher altitudes, the species of plants and animals that live on mountains change with the altitude. Mountains are divided into life zones according to the plant species living at different altitudes. A mountain may have four different life zones from bottom to top: the foothills zone, the montane (mon-TAYN) zone, the subalpine zone, and the alpine zone. The foothills zone has the driest, warmest weather. At the other extreme, the alpine zone is the highest, wettest, and coldest life zone.

The higher the life zone, the shorter the growing season, or the part of the year when the weather is warm enough for plants to grow. In the foothills, the growing season may last four months or more. But in the bitter land of the alpine zone, the growing season lasts just two months.

Short pines, junipers, and oaks, seen here in the Sierra Nevada Mountains in California, are common foothill trees in the American West.

Spruce and fir trees can survive the long, cold winters in the subalpine zone of many western mountain ranges.

The foothills of America's western mountains have dry soil. Here, short species of pine, juniper, and oak are most common, because these scrub trees need less water than the taller trees at higher altitudes.

Moving uphill to the montane zone, often a heavily forested area on a mountain, there may be a variety of trees. Ponderosa pines and Douglas fir are two of the most common montane species in the West. They need more moisture than trees found in the foothills, but can live with a shorter growing season.

Higher up is the subalpine zone, where the coniferous forests are much like those in the snowy lands of the far North. This zone is wetter and colder, and has a shorter growing season than the lower life zones. Species of spruce, fir, and pine trees do well in this zone.

America's eastern mountains are generally wetter than those of the West. The extra water means that moisture-loving, broad-leaved trees are more common than conifers. However, eastern mountain winters can be long and cold on the higher peaks. Therefore, as in the West, cold-tolerant conifers are more common in high-altitude areas.

If you climb high enough through a subalpine forest, the trees eventually disappear. The place where the subalpine forest ends and the high-elevation alpine zone begins is called the tree line. Above the tree line, the winds are among the world's strongest. Subfreezing temperatures occur nightly, even during the summer. Alpine zone weather is so cold and windy that most young trees die during their first year.

The altitude of the tree line gets lower as you travel northward into areas with colder climates and shorter growing seasons. In the Colorado Rockies the forest ends at about 11,000 feet (3,353 m) up, while in the Canadian Rockies—much farther north—the tree line is at about 7,000 feet (2,134 m). In the far North, above the Arctic Circle, tree growth is impossible at any altitude.

The altitude of the tree line may also vary on a single mountain. Slopes facing south receive more sunlight and are warmer than north-facing slopes. As a result, subalpine forests grow at higher altitudes on south-facing slopes than on north-facing slopes.

Patches of krummholz and a flag tree grow at the tree line in Colorado's Sangre de Cristo Mountains.

The severe wind and cold keep the trees at the tree line short. Many tree line trees have odd shapes because of the extreme weather. Some of these strange little trees form miniature forests called krummholz (KRUM-holtz). Krummholz is a German word meaning "crooked wood."

For protection from the weather, krummholz trees grow close together, like bushes in a hedge. If a krummholz tree grows taller than its neighbors, it will only sprout branches on its leeward side; the icy winds block growth on the windward side. These strange-looking trees with branches on only one side are called flag trees. Their name comes from their shape—they look like flags blowing in the wind.

The altitude of the tree line changes from place to place on a mountain due to the differences in the local climate.

Trees that grow at the tree line, such as this bristlecone pine, often have strange shapes due to the severe winds and weather at high altitudes.

Alpine tundra occurs throughout America's northern mountain ranges, from Alaska to New Hampshire.

Alpine weather is hard on plants. Yet some species do grow in the alpine zone above the tree line. They are part of a special environment called the alpine tundra. Most tundra plants grow to less than one foot tall because of the wind. As the wind blows, the air closest to the ground scrapes against the earth and slows down. So the wind blows more slowly close to the ground than it does higher up. By staying short, alpine tundra plants avoid the worst gusts.

Many alpine tundra plants have lowland relatives, but these species are often very different from their high-altitude cousins. The alpine sunflower, for example, has a big yellow flower like other sunflowers. However, it is short—no more than a foot (30.48 cm) tall—while its lowland relatives can grow to more than six feet (1.83 m). Like many tundra plants, the alpine sunflower's stem and leaves are hairy. The hairs help block the wind.

Tundra plants often have chemicals in them that keep the water in their stems and leaves from turning into ice. These chemicals act like the antifreeze that prevents the water in a car's radiator from freezing during the winter. Snow may also keep tundra plants from freezing. A layer of snow acts like a blanket, protecting the plants from the cold air.

The tundra's brief, eight-week growing season means the plants here grow slowly—just a fraction of an inch each year. It may take some species 20 years to put out their first flower. But there is life and growth in every mountain zone—even in the bitter alpine tundra.

Why is the alpine sunflower so much shorter than its relatives in the lowlands?

CHAPTER SIX

Horns, Hooves, Fur, and Feathers

Mountain goats in Olympic National Park in Washington use their hooves for gripping and climbing across sharp rocks.

Animals found in the lowlands, such as bears, squirrels, and mice, may also live in mountain forests. However, many creatures visit the alpine zone only during the warm months and escape below the tree line before winter. Deer and elk graze on the tundra but head downhill at summer's end. Even most bighorn sheep, symbols of the high mountains, move to the lower slopes when snow falls. Those animals that do brave alpine winters have special ways to stay alive.

Most high mountain birds fly south, or to lower altitudes, before their food supply becomes snow-covered. Only the white-tailed ptarmigan (TAR-mi-gin) remains in the alpine zone all year. Ptarmigans survive on leaves that cling to bushes sticking above the snow.

The white-tailed ptarmigan's white winter feathers are falling out and are being replaced by gray and brown summer feathers.

The pika may look like a mouse, but it's actually related to rabbits.

Marmots (MAR-motz) and pikas (PY-kuhz) are two small, common alpine tundra animals. The marmot, about the size of a groundhog, eats all summer and enters a deep sleep-like state, called hibernation during the winter. But the rat-sized pika stays awake through the winter, safe and warm in its home beneath the rocks and snow. It eats plants it stored in the summer.

The mountain goat also has special ways to survive at high elevations. Its white coat is thick and warm. Its body is thin, so it can fit on narrow ledges. Its feet are built for gripping the rocks. No other large animal climbs so well. Climbing is the mountain goat's best defense. If a mountain lion attacks, the mountain goat dashes up the nearest cliff where its enemy can't follow.

CHAPTER SEVEN

Mountains of Change

In 2002, the many paved roads cutting through Yosemite National Park brought over 3 million people to the Sierra Nevada Mountains.

When America was young, only a handful of tough mountaineers traveled into the high country. The logger's ax rarely cut into the trees of the montane or subalpine forests. And the farmers plow barely touched the rocky, mountain soils. But the modern road-maker's bulldozer is another story. Roads now crisscross America's mountains. As a result, the number of hikers, hunters, skiers, miners, ranchers, loggers, and home-builders using the mountains has skyrocketed. The wild mountain scenery that so many people love is changing fast and disappearing.

Even people who never visit the mountains may use them without realizing it. Mountain forests and the alpine tundra serve as natural water towers. They store water from rain and melting snow like huge sponges and then release water slowly to the lowlands. However, when the forests are cut down or the tundra is damaged, most of the water washes down the slopes, which causes flooding. Then later, during dryer times, there's less water left for people to use.

Also, when a mountain's protective trees and plants are removed, the soil lies open to erosion. Soil sediments wash into clear mountain streams, making the water muddy. The mud harms our drinking water and makes it hard for salmon, trout, and other fish to survive.

Besides being important sources of water, lumber, and minerals, mountains provide peace of mind for many people. In the words of the poet Lord Byron, "High mountains are a feeling, but the hum of human cities torture." The number of people living in America's mountains is still small compared to other parts of the continent. But the number of people who need the mountains is great—even if they live far away.

The water in this stream, in New York's Catskill Mountains, may eventually be used by people many miles away.

GLOSSARY

alpine tundra area high in the mountains where the weather is too cold for tree growth and the plants are short

alpine zone the part of a mountain above the tree line

altitude distance or height above sea level

asthenosphere layer of the Earth below the lithosphere, which is between about 60 miles (100 km) to 220 miles (350 km) from the Earth's surface and which is made of semisolid rock and magma

basalt dark igneous rock often formed from hardened lava

basin lowered area in the Earth's crust, often lying between fault-block mountain ranges

butte high land formation with very steep sides and a flat top smaller than that of a mesa

cordillera group of mountain systems

crater volcano opening from which lava and volcanic ash spew during volcanic activity

crust outermost layer of the Earth within the lithosphere

divide high area separating two drainage systems

dome mountain portion of the Earth's crust that bulges upward due to the magma underneath, and that forms a high dome

drainage system stream or river and all the streams or rivers flowing into it, which together carry water out of a certain area of land

elevation height above sea level

erosion wearing away of soil and rock by wind, water, ice, and other natural forces

erosion mountains high areas of land that remain as mountains after a plateau is eroded away

fault crack in the Earth's crust along which the blocks on either side of the crack move in different directions

fault-block mountain mountain formed when the Earth's crust breaks, forms a block, and then tilts up

folded mountains mountains formed from the large folds of the Earth's crust that are created when one tectonic plate slides beneath another tectonic plate

foothills hilly region at the base of a mountain range

foothills zone lowest-altitude mountain life zone

glacier large mass of ice moving slowly down a mountain or across a land surface

granite hard, igneous rock usually formed from magma and with large amounts of the minerals quartz and feldspar

hot spot an area of the Earth's surface that is above a mass of magma, which rises up from the asthenosphere

ice age period of time during which the climate becomes colder and glaciers form to cover much of the Earth

igneous type of rock made from magma or lava

lava hot, liquid rock that flows out onto the Earth's surface

leeward   facing away from the direction the wind is blowing from

limestone   sedimentary rock consisting mainly of the mineral calcite

lithosphere   solid outer layer of the Earth, about 60 miles (100 km) thick

magma   hot, liquid rock inside the Earth

mesa   elevated piece of land with at least one steep side and a flat top that is smaller than the top of a plateau but larger than that of a butte

metamorphic rock   new rock created from already existing rock as a result of great heat or pressure

mineral   natural substance that forms rocks

molten rock   rock that is so hot it is a liquid

montane zone   mountain life zone with a temperature range, growing season, and altitude that falls between those of the foothills and subalpine zones

moraine   mound of sediment dropped by a glacier

mountain range   one or more closely spaced mountains or ridges related in the way they were formed

mountain system   group of mountain ranges within a certain area

plateau   area of level, raised land with at least one steep side

plate tectonics   theory that the lithosphere is divided into separate plates that move slowly on the Earth's surface

sandstone   sedimentary rock formed from sand

sediment   particles such as rocks, pebbles, sand, and silt that may be carried by water, wind, or glaciers

shale   sedimentary rock formed from clay, silt, or mud

shield   large area of hard rock exposed by erosion that is part of the foundation rock of a continent

silt   particles smaller than the finest sand but larger than particles of clay

snowfield   area of snow that doesn't melt during the summer

subalpine zone   mountain life zone with a temperature range, growing season, and altitude that falls between those of the montane and alpine zones

summit   highest point of a mountain, hill, or other high landform

tree line   place on a mountain beyond which only sparse trees, krummholz, or tundra exist

volcano   hill or mountain made up of rock formed from lava that moved from the Earth's interior onto the surface

water vapor   water in the form of gas

windward   facing toward the direction the wind is blowing from

INDEX